The Mirror and the Mind

Unraveling the Lacanian Subject

Freudian Trips

Copyright Page

This book is a work of non-fiction. Unless otherwise noted, the author and the publisher make no explicit guarantees as to the accuracy of the information contained in this book and will not be held responsible for any errors or omissions.

Published by Omniterra Media Inc

First Edition

Visit the author's website at www.freudiantrips.com

Disclaimer

The views and opinions expressed in this book are those of the author(s) and do not necessarily reflect the official policy or position of any other agency, organization, employer, or company. The contents of this book are for informational and educational purposes only and are not intended to serve as professional advice, diagnosis, or treatment.

The information provided in this book is believed to be accurate and reliable as of the date of publication. However, it may include some errors or inaccuracies, and no warranty or guarantee is provided regarding the accuracy, timeliness, or applicability of the content.

Readers are encouraged to consult with professional philosophers, educators, or other qualified professionals where appropriate for personalized advice. The author(s) and publisher shall not be liable for any loss, damage, or harm caused or alleged to be caused, directly or indirectly, by the information or ideas contained, suggested, or referenced in this book.

By reading this book, the reader acknowledges and agrees that they are solely responsible for how they interpret and apply the information contained herein.

This book may also include references to other works, studies, and sources. These references are provided for further reading and exploration and do not imply endorsement or validation of the specific theories, viewpoints, or interpretations presented in those works.

Introduction: Freud's Legacy and Lacan's Challenge

When we think of psychology, one name usually comes to mind: Sigmund Freud. He revolutionized the way we think about ourselves. Freud believed that below the surface of our everyday thoughts lies a hidden world – the unconscious. This realm is filled with buried desires, forgotten memories, and powerful urges that secretly shape who we are.

Freud's ideas were, of course, controversial, but they left an undeniable mark. However, along came a thinker named Jacques Lacan, a French psychoanalyst who both admired Freud and thought his theories didn't go far enough. Lacan saw the power of our deepest desires, but he also believed that Freud didn't fully understand the force that shapes those desires: language itself.

Lacan was a fascinating guy. He was incredibly smart, a bit of a showman, and he loved to stir things up. His writings are notoriously complex, filled with twists and turns that might make your head spin. But, beneath that difficult surface lies a set of ideas that offer a new window into the way our minds work, and perhaps even why we sometimes act in ways we don't fully understand.

The Challenge of Understanding Lacan

Let's be honest – trying to grasp Lacan is like taking on an advanced puzzle. Don't get discouraged if it seems overwhelming at first. The goal of this book is to break down his ideas into clear pieces, helping you see how they connect to your own life and reveal something new about yourself.

Think of it like this: Freud was the explorer who ventured into the hidden depths of the mind. Lacan is the cartographer who tries to draw a map of that strange territory, a map drawn with language and the strange logic of the unconscious. We'll take this journey together, one step at a time.

Chapter 1: The Shattered Reflection – Discovering the "I"

Imagine being a baby. The world is a swirl of sensations, faces, and strange objects. You don't yet understand there's a "you" separate from the blanket you love or your mom's warm smile. Then, one day, something incredible happens – you catch sight of yourself in a mirror.

That moment, according to Jacques Lacan, isn't just about babies learning to recognize their own faces. It's the birth of something called the ego, your sense of "I." But here's the twist: Lacan believed that the "I" you see in that mirror is a bit of an illusion. Let me explain.

The Whole vs. The Fragmented

Before the mirror, your experience as a baby is a bit chaotic. You may sometimes feel hungry, sometimes happy, sometimes unsure. Your body doesn't feel like a neatly packaged whole. But the image in the mirror seems different! It looks like a complete, contained little person.

Lacan says this is where the seed of the ego is planted. You start to identify with that image, believing that it represents your true self. The problem is, it's like a snapshot frozen in time. The real you is always moving, changing, and feeling all sorts of things, not that perfect reflection.

Enter Fantasy

So, why do we cling to the image in the mirror? Because it offers a comforting story. Instead of the messy, ever-changing reality, this "I" feels solid and certain. This is where fantasy kicks in. You start building an ideal picture of yourself based on what you saw, and maybe you start aspiring to always be like that well-behaved, cute kid in the reflection.

The Incomplete Self

The ego, that sense of "I," is essential. It helps us navigate the world. But, according to Lacan, it's also a source of constant tension. We're always trying to live up to that perfect image, yet deep down we know it's impossible. The real self, with all its imperfections and messy desires, keeps bubbling under the surface.

The Mirror Stage in Your Life

Think about times you've compared yourself to others – on social media, at school, wherever. That's your ego at work, measuring your "real" self against an ideal image. The mirror stage isn't just a baby thing, it's the story of how we constantly construct and struggle with our own identities.

Chapter 2: Decoding Your Mind's Secret Map

Get ready for a mind-bending adventure! Imagine your mind is like a vast, unexplored territory. Jacques Lacan believed this territory could be roughly divided into three zones, each with its own unique landscape and hidden rules. He called these zones the Imaginary, the Symbolic, and the Real.

Zone 1: The Imaginary – It's All About the Image

Think back to the mirror stage we talked about. That's where the Imaginary begins. It's the realm of images, appearances, and how we see ourselves. Our egos live here! The Imaginary is like a giant movie screen inside your head, constantly playing scenes of who you are, who you want to be, and how you relate to others.

Narcissism: The Imaginary's Dark Side

Remember Narcissus, the guy from Greek mythology who fell in love with his reflection in the water? That's where the term narcissism comes from. It's an extreme form of getting stuck in the Imaginary. You become obsessed with your image, with creating the perfect version of yourself, but the catch is the more you chase that perfection, the further you get from your real, imperfect self.

Zone 2: The Symbolic – The Power of Words

The Symbolic is all about language, rules, and the larger social world we live in. Think of it like an invisible network of meanings and codes that shape how we understand everything. When you were born, you weren't just dropped into a neutral world; you were born into a world filled with words and pre-existing ideas.

The Rules of the Game: The Symbolic shapes how we think, what we value, even what we find attractive. It's like the rulebook of society, and we spend our lives unconsciously playing by those rules without even realizing it.

Zone 3: The Real – Where Language Breaks Down

The Real is the wild, untamed part of the mind that resists easy explanations. It's the realm of intense emotions, primal urges, and sometimes traumatic experiences that are so overwhelming, they can't be neatly put into words. Think of it like a hidden, rumbling volcano beneath the surface of our conscious minds.

The Unexplainable: The Real is a reminder that we aren't always in control. It's where our deepest fears and anxieties lurk, and it can sometimes erupt into our lives in unexpected ways.

The Neverending Road Trip

The thing about these three orders is that they're not separate islands within you. Your mind is in constant motion, shifting between them. Sometimes you're lost in the Imaginary, obsessing over your image. Other times you're navigating the Symbolic, trying to figure out the social rules. And sometimes, a glimpse of the Real shakes everything up.

Understanding these orders gives you a new way to understand yourself: your fantasies, your relationships, and those moments when you feel like a stranger in your own mind.

Chapter 3: The Curious Case of What We Really Want

Have you ever wanted something so badly, only to find that once you got it, it... wasn't all that satisfying? Or felt a twinge of envy seeing the perfect life someone flaunts online, even though you know it might not be real? This strange puzzle of desire is exactly what Jacques Lacan wanted to unravel.

The Desire Machine

Lacan had this famous (and somewhat confusing) statement: "Man's desire is the desire of the Other." But what the heck does that even mean? Put simply, it's about how our deepest desires are never just about the things themselves.

The "Other": This isn't just about other people. It's a bigger concept. The "Other" can represent society, expectations we feel we need to meet, or even some fantasy version of ourselves.

Beyond Basic Needs: Think about a baby. Sure, they need food and comfort. But they also crave their mom's attention and love. Desire, according to Lacan, is like that. It's not just about survival; it's about wanting to feel recognized, seen, and whole. The catch is that wholeness is always slipping through our fingers.

The Trap of Lack

Here's the tricky part: Lacan believed that there's a fundamental lack at the core of who we are, a missing piece we're forever trying to fill. This is where desire is born. We want the shiny new toy, the perfect relationship, the dream job... thinking that thing will finally complete us. Spoiler alert: it never does.

Fantasyland: To keep that desire machine running, we use the power of fantasy. That perfect life you envy on Instagram? It's a fantasy. The image of yourself you keep striving towards? Also a bit of a fantasy. We use these to cover up that uncomfortable feeling of lack.

So Why Do We Keep Desiring?

Because desire, even with the frustration it brings, is what keeps us going. It propels us to learn, create, and connect. The trick, according to Lacan, isn't to get rid of desire, but to understand where it's truly coming from. When we start to unmask those fantasies tied to our deepest desires, we can start making choices that are truly our own, rather than simply chasing echoes of the "Other."

Chapter 4: Your Mind's Secret Language Club

If someone told you that your unconscious mind has its own secret language, you might think they're a bit off their rocker. But that's more or less what Jacques Lacan argued, and it turns out he might have been onto something.

Freud's Basement of the Mind

Remember Freud? He saw the unconscious as a hidden storage locker – full of repressed memories, unacceptable urges, and all the stuff you'd rather not think about. For Freud, it was wild, chaotic, a bit like a swirling soup of hidden impulses.

Lacan's Twist: It's All About Language

Lacan took Freud's idea and gave it a remix. He said, "Hold on, the unconscious isn't just a jumble of impulses; it has structure, like a language." Now, this doesn't mean there are little words and sentences floating around in there, but rather, the way your unconscious mind works has similarities to the ways in which language functions.

The Language Toolkit

Let's break down a few key ideas:

- **Signifier vs. Signified:** Every word is a signifier, a sound or image that stands for something. But the meaning, the signified, isn't fixed. Think of the word "love" – it can bring up all sorts of personal meanings and associations in your mind. In your unconscious, Lacan believed the same thing is happening – images, memories, and feelings act like signifiers that have slippery meanings.
- **Metaphor and Metonymy:** Remember these from English class? Metaphor is about substitution ("love is a battlefield"), metonymy is about a part standing for the whole (saying "the White House decided" instead of "the President decided"). Lacan believed our unconscious works in the same way, constantly substituting one thing for another and making connections based on association rather than logic.

Decoding Your Mental Messages

Why does this matter? Picture your mind as an iceberg. Your conscious mind is just the tip, but below the surface is a vast hidden landscape. The language of the unconscious reveals your true desires, hidden fears, and the stuff you've buried deep down long ago.

Lacan thought that this unconscious language slips out in our everyday lives:

- **Slips of the Tongue:** Ever accidentally called your partner by your ex's name? Freud was all over that, but Lacan would see that as your unconscious language making an unexpected cameo appearance.
- **Dreams:** Wild, nonsensical dream plots? Lacan viewed them as coded messages from your unconscious, using its own metaphorical language.

Understanding these linguistic tricks your unconscious mind plays can open a whole new window into understanding yourself on a deeper level.

Chapter 5: The Talking Cure, Lacanian Style

If you picture therapy the classic way – a patient lying on a couch, a therapist taking notes – you're in for a surprise with Lacanian psychoanalysis. Lacan flipped the script, focusing on the patient's language, unexpected word choices, and seemingly offhand remarks as clues to their deeper unconscious world.

The Speech Detective

Traditional psychoanalysis often focuses on delving into your past, unpacking childhood experiences. A Lacanian analyst does this too, but with a twist: they're less interested in figuring out why you are the way you are, and more focused on how your speech patterns in the present moment reveal those hidden desires and conflicts bubbling under the surface.

Wordplay and Freudian Slips: Remember how we talked about the unconscious being structured like a language? In a Lacanian session, every slip of the tongue, every turn of phrase, is analyzed. It's a bit like a linguistic treasure hunt. The analyst is listening for those moments where your unconscious tries to break into your conscious speech.

Cutting Things Short: Another unique feature of Lacanian analysis are the sessions themselves. They might be super short compared to traditional therapy! The idea is to shake things up a bit and prevent you from getting too comfortable with a rambling narrative about your life. The surprise can jolt the unconscious into making an appearance.

The Dynamic Duo: Transference and Countertransference

Here's where things get extra interesting.

- **Transference:** This happens in all therapy. It's when you unconsciously project feelings and past relationships onto your therapist. But, for a Lacanian analyst, this isn't a problem to be fixed, it's a playground to explore your unconscious desires.
- **Countertransference:** This is about the therapist's own feelings and reactions towards the patient. A Lacanian views their own emotional responses as important clues to what's going on beneath the surface of the patient's words.

The Goal? Not Always a Neat Solution

Lacanian analysis isn't about giving you a step-by-step guide to fixing your problems. It's about helping you confront the fundamental split within yourself, recognize the illusions of your ego, and get more in touch with your true desires, even if they're messy and contradictory.

It's a therapy for those who don't want easy answers but are brave enough to go on a deep and sometimes confusing journey into their own unconscious landscapes.

Chapter 6: The Echoes of Lacan – Controversy and Creativity

Jacques Lacan was more than just a therapist with unusual theories. His ideas rippled far beyond the world of psychology, leaving a mark that is both admired and highly controversial. Let's explore his far-reaching impact and take a look at why he remains a hotly debated figure.

Lacan the Philosopher

Lacan's take on the unconscious wasn't just about therapy, it sparked new ways of thinking about who we are as individuals and as a society. Philosophers became fascinated by his ideas about language, desire, and the illusion of a stable self. They saw how deeply his work questioned basic assumptions about how we make meaning of the world.

Lights, Camera, Lacan!

Think about your favorite movies, especially psychological thrillers or twisty dramas where the line between reality and fantasy blurs. Filmmakers found inspiration in Lacan's theories about the power of the image, the slippery nature of identity, and the dark side of desire. His ideas gave them tools to explore the hidden corners of their characters' minds and make the audience question what they were seeing.

Diving into Literature with Lacan

Ever read a book and realize there's way more going on than just the plot on the surface? Literary critics armed with Lacan's theories took a deep dive into texts, looking for hidden patterns of language, repressed desires lurking within characters, and how the very way a story is told can shape the reader's understanding.

Lacan and Feminism: A Complicated Relationship

Feminist thinkers have a love-hate relationship with Lacan. Some find his focus on the role of language in shaping our identities empowering. It can expose the ways that traditional gender roles get encoded into how we think and act.

However, others point out that Lacan often seems to center male experience, and his theories can sometimes reinforce stereotypical ideas about women. This tension highlights that even seemingly "neutral" theories can carry hidden biases.

The Criticism: Too Complicated, Too Sexist?

Lacan has been called everything from a genius to a charlatan. Here are some of the main criticisms:

- Obscure: Let's face it, his writing is tough. Critics argue that his use of complex language makes his ideas inaccessible and masks a lack of real substance.

- Sexist: Some accuse Lacan of perpetuating outdated ideas about gender, viewing women primarily through the lens of male desire.
- Anti-humanist: Critics say his view of the fragmented self, trapped within language, is a bleak one that ignores human potential and free will.

The Legacy

Whether you embrace or despise him, there's no denying Lacan's impact. He forced us to think differently about the deepest workings of our minds, the power of language, and how society shapes our sense of self. Even his critics wrestle with his ideas, showing that sometimes the most provocative thinkers are the ones that keep the conversation going long after they're gone.

Conclusion: The Enigma of Lacan – Enduring Questions and Unsettled Thoughts

Jacques Lacan was a whirlwind of ideas, shaking up everything we thought we knew about our own minds. While his writing might make you want to tear your hair out at times, there's no doubt his theories leave you with some lingering questions. Let's recap some of his most important ideas and why we're still talking about them today.

Lacan's Key Takeaways

- The Mirror and the Illusion of Self: Lacan reminded us that our identity isn't a given. We construct it in relation to images and ideals, but there's always a gap between our ego and the messy, ever-changing reality of who we are.
- Desire – It's Not What You Think: Desire isn't just about wanting stuff. At its core, it's about a yearning for recognition, a never-ending search for that missing piece that will make us feel whole.

- The Power (and Limits) of Language: Lacan showed us that language doesn't just describe the world, it shapes the world. He highlighted how the very way we think is influenced by deep structures of language and societal expectations.
- The Unconscious Speaks: While Freud uncovered the unconscious, Lacan argued that it functions like a language, filled with symbols, slips of the tongue, and hidden codes waiting to be deciphered.

Why Lacan Still Matters

In our age of selfies, social media comparison, and relentless quests for perfection, Lacan's focus on the constructed ego feels more relevant than ever. His emphasis on the deceptive power of images resonates in a world obsessed with appearances.

His ideas also force us to confront the limits of our conscious control. Our deepest desires, our anxieties, and even our own words can sometimes betray hidden aspects of ourselves, revealing the constant struggle between our conscious minds and the shadowy forces of the unconscious.

Challenges and the Future

Lacan's complex theories continue to spark both fascination and fierce debate. It's important to grapple with his potential blind spots, like questions about gender or accusations of overlooking the importance of real-world experiences.

Yet, the very act of wrestling with his work sparks crucial conversations. Lacan might not give us easy instructions for how to live, but he invites us to look behind the certainties we take for granted, asking us to question the stories we tell ourselves about ourselves. There's a strange power in realizing that we might be more mysterious to ourselves than we like to admit. And that kind of self-exploration is perhaps the most fascinating and unsettling journey of all.

About Freudian Trips

Welcome to Freudian Trips, your dedicated platform for diving deep into the world of psychology. We are more than just a YouTube channel or a book publisher. We are a beacon of enlightenment, making complex psychological concepts accessible and engaging for all.

Our YouTube channel is a rich repository of psychology made simple. We take the profound and often complex ideas from the world of psychology and break them down into digestible, easy-to-understand content. From the foundational theories of Freud to the cognitive insights of Piaget, we cover a broad spectrum of psychological schools and thoughts, making psychology accessible to everyone, regardless of their background or prior knowledge.

As a book publisher, we take the same approach, transforming intricate psychological theories into comprehensible narratives. Our books are not just collections of words, but vessels of wisdom that make psychology approachable and relatable. We believe that psychology should not be confined to academic circles, but should be available to all who seek to understand the human mind and behavior.

At Freudian Trips, we believe in the power of curiosity and the pursuit of knowledge. We are here to stoke the fires of your curiosity, to guide you on your intellectual journey, and to help you navigate the fascinating world of psychology.

If you are someone who is not afraid to question, to explore, and to learn, then you are in the right place. Join us on this journey of exploration, as we make psychology easy to understand, one concept at a time.

Be sure to visit our Youtube channel at:
www.freudiantrips.com/youtube

You can also visit us on the web at www.freudiantrips.com

Welcome to The Freudian Trip community. Stay curious. Stay enlightened.